The Next Step in Investing:

Revenue Based Financing

"LUNI" LIBES

LUNARMOBISCUIT PUBLISHING

Edited by Monica Aufrecht
Cover sketches by designed by Freepik

Published by Lunarmobiscuit Publishing

PRINT ISBN 978-0-9980947-9-3

BEFORE YOU BEGIN

IS THIS BOOK FOR YOU?

THIS BOOK IS for both entrepreneurs and investors. This book debunks myths about the best way to finance startups and small business. This book also presents an alternative way to fund those companies.

There is no way to explain how startups are financed without using jargon from the world of venture capital. But don't worry if you are not fluent in that language. I'll explain it all in plain English.

"REVENUE" AND "ROYALTY"

DEPENDING ON WHERE you live, investors might refer to concepts discussed in this book as: "revenue-based financing," "royalty-based financing," "preferred-redeemable equity," "demand dividends," "structured exits," or some other term. The investor world has not yet settled on a single name. I prefer the term "revenue-based financing," shortened to the acronym **RBF**.

"TYPICALLY"

THIS BOOK IS going to make a lot of definitive statements. E.g., "startup investors do not loan money to startup companies." Whenever you see such statements, add the word "typically" or "usually" in your mind, as there are exceptions to every otherwise hard and fast rule.

THE NEXT STEP IN INVESTING

CONTENTS

THE EMPEROR, CLOTHES, AND YOU

A.K.A. YOU ARE DOING IT ALL WRONG

INVESTING ALL WRONG

IT SEEMS CRAZY and presumptuous to say that the hundred billion dollar startup investing industry does business all wrong, but nonetheless it is true.

Not that investing in startups is itself wrong. History has clearly shown there is value in these investments both for entrepreneurs and investors.

Rather, it is wrong in the manner of Hans Christian Andersen's story "The Emperor's New Clothes." In that story, the emperor parades around town wearing an invisible "suit," with his nobles and all the press touting how wonderful and splendid his clothing is because no one wants to admit they cannot see the clothes.

NAKED EMPERORS?

The naked emperor metaphor is not a perfect fit here, as the players doing startup financing wrong are not the decades-old, well-proven venture capital funds like Sequoia, Kleiner Perkins, and Bessemer, nor the newer additions to the top 10 VC fund lists like Andreessen Horowitz, Founders Fund, and Union Square.

In the venture capital industry (a.k.a. the asset class known as *early-stage private equity*), the top 10 VC funds are highly successful. The top 10% of VC funds earn a lot of money for their investors. It the other 90% of venture capital funds that this book applies to, along with the tens of thousands of Angel investors who look to replicate the success of the top VCs.

VENTURE HISTORY

The underlying problem discussed in this book comes from

"traditional" startup investing. This history seems ancient and fundamental, but in reality the industry truly began as recently as the 1970s, and only grew to any significant size in the early 1990s.

There were capitalists funding the industrial revolution in the early 1800s, and capitalists along side JP Morgan funding railroads, steel, and electrification in the late 1800s and early 20th Century, but their model of investing was different from modern venture capital.

There were also a few pioneers in modern venture capital before the 1970s, but it wasn't until 1972 that Kleiner Perkins and Sequoia first opened shop on Sand Hill Road in Palo Alto, California, an area first named "Silicon Valley" in a newspaper article in 1971. (Sand Hill Road is still the epicenter of venture capital today and the most prestigious address in the industry.)

In 1974, the Employee Retirement Income Security Act (ERISA) allowed pension funds to invest in privately held companies, and in 1978 they amended the regulations to make it clear that pension funds could invest in early stage private equity. This opened the floodgates of capital into the sector, at first with hundreds of millions of dollars per year, and then growing to tens of billions by the dot-com bubble in the late 1990s.

It was in those decades of the 70s, 80s, and 90s when the structure of modern venture capital investments was formed, specifically the structure of *preferred equity*. Later in the book we'll talk about the details, but in short, the key idea is that the investor provides capital to the company and then receives a return on that investment when the company either gets acquired or "goes public." (This is the same as equity ownership, but with additional *preferences* over the founders' and employees' equity).

This same structure, down to the details of the preferences on the equity, is copied by nearly every venture capital fund since 1972, and copied as best they can by Angel investors too.

That is the flaw. The structure works for Sequoia and Kleiner Perkins and is working for Andreessen Horowitz and Union Square, but, in general, it is the wrong structure for 99.9% of all potential startup investments.

The emperors are fully clothed, and everyone around them is naked!

(IM)PATIENT CAPITAL

FOR 99.9% OF STARTUPS the flaw in the relationship between entrepreneurs and investors is the structure of the investments, not the business plan or execution of that plan. Again, in the simplest form, venture capital investments since the 1970s have traditionally taken the form of preferred equity, where the investor buys shares in the company, then holds those shares until another buyer comes along. In startup investing, such an acquisition is called an "exit."

Here in the 21st Century, if a buyer ever comes along, it is most often a much larger company, one that was itself a startup a decade or two ago and is now looking to continue its fast grow. On a rare occasion that buyer is an anonymous buyer on a stock exchange, after the company has been successful enough to "go public," i.e., issue an "initial public offering" (an "IPO") and get listed on the New York Stock Exchange or NASDAQ.

Either way, the pattern to notice is that the investor hands over money to the company, then waits for an unknown period of time for news of the outcome. (During that wait the company could ask for more money in exchange for more shares, but those "rounds" of investment typically take this same basic form, and don't necessarily speed up the overall timeline nor the overall outcome.)

Talk to the 80% of venture capital funds that are not successful or talk to most Angel investors and you tend to hear the same lament:

"I don't have any exits."

Ask for details and you'll discover that some of the companies they invested in have shut down. Startup death is in fact an exit, but the type that investors don't like to talk about. Those are the losses or "zeros."

If the investors have had some exits, press harder and you'll often find that these are "aquihires," wherein the acquirer purchased the company in order to hire the team, not to get the customers of the company. Aquihires often involve a price equal to or less than the amount of capital the investors invested. Thus, these are also often losses, or at best a "1x" return of capital.

When investors dream about exits they are dreaming about a return of at least ten times their money back. A "**10x**."

The dream of the 10x is what motivates startup investors to invest. It is the core reason they structure their investment as preferred equity, and the fundamental flaw in the behavior of startup investors.

THE PROVERBIAL 10X

ODDLY, WHEN YOU talk to a startup venture capitalists or Angel investor and ask them how much they expect to earn on their last investment, the answer will inevitably be "10x or more." Why? Where does this magic number come from and what does it really mean?

This general response is even more odd once you realize the answer has nothing to do with what company they invested in. It doesn't matter if it was another software-as-a-service, a company using drones to replant forests, or a company with self-driving cars. The answer is always 10x. Isn't that strange?

Actually, it is not strange at all once you unpack all the unstated assumptions hiding within that very shorthand term, *10x*.

EQUITY INVESTING

Let's step back to look at the details of how startup investors make their investments, which is by buying **preferred shares** a.k.a. buying **equity**. (The word "preferred" refers to the fact that the investor's shares come with a set of terms that place "preferences" on their shares over the "common" shares owned by the founders. The details of the preferences will be discussed later in the book.)

For now, let's focus on the money. The total amount of cash provided by the investor equals the number of shares multiplied by the share price. Let's call the total amount of cash **$D**.

In exchange for the cash, the company makes no promise to pay any of the money back to the investor. Instead, the expectation by both the investor and the startup founders is that the company will grow in value and that sometime, many years later, the company will have an **exit** (be acquired or go public).

In the case of an acquisition, within 30 days of the transaction, the investor receives a check or bank wire with a percentage of the acquisition price, based roughly on the number of shares owned at that time (Roughly, as the details can get complicated, and thus are described later). In the case of an IPO, the investor's shares can be sold on the public stock exchange 180 days after the IPO (the waiting period is called a "lock up" and is a regulatory requirement).

Either way, soon after an exit, the investor knows how much money he/she made on that investment.

An exit is considered successful for the investor when the total cash returned to the investor is much more than the investor provided to the company. It could be five times the initial investment. Or ten times. Or for the early Facebook and Google investors, fifty times. For a less successful exit, the investor might simply get their money back: their return from the exit is exactly the same amount of cash as their initial investment was, which, if you remember your grade school math, is the same as one times $D. They call this "1x" (pronounced "one ex"). And for companies that run out of money and shut down, no money at all is returned, which, again from grade school math, is zero times $D. They call this "Zero ex" and most investors don't like to talk about these.

Given these values have a large range, investors talk about them as multiples of $D rather than percentages. Thus "**10x**" simply means the investor received ten times more money back than was originally invested. "2x" means they doubled their investment. "1x" means they got their money back.

ONE IN 10X

Earning ten times your money seems like a great plan. Who wouldn't want to turn $10,000 into $100,000, $500,000 into $5 million, or $7 million into $70 million? That sure sounds better than earning 0.1% interest in a savings account or the historic 7% annual average from the stock market.

What you have to understand is that most startup investments don't returning anything close to 10x. In fact, even for successful, full-time, professional venture capitalists and for the most experienced Angels, a good result is that only **1 in 10** investments returns 10x or more.

Below is what a successful startup portfolio looks like (with a big thanks to my friend and Seattle "Super Angel" Geoff Entress who explained this to my MBA students). Let's break it down line by line.

Angel/VC returns per 10 investments		
1/10 "Home Run"		>10x
2/10 "Double/Triples"		5x
3/10 "Singles"		1x
4/10 Zeros		0x
Average (10%*10x)+(20%*5x)+(30%*1x)		**2.3x**

First, in the header, note this is "per ten investments." A venture capital fund typically invests into fifteen to twenty different startups and Angels are told to similarly make at least fifteen investments, ideally more. To keep the math simple, the table looks at an arbitrary collection of ten of those investments.

Next, note that the unspoken assumption is that each of those ten investments had an expectation of returning at least a 10x. Investors who follow this traditional 10x investing model often talk about how every startup needs to "swing for the fences" or how the only option is to "go big or go home." You cannot earn an average of 2.3x as listed in the table if one of your investments is a loan to your sister-in-law for her business, or is some equity you received in exchange for being a startup advisor without other payment.

In this analysis, there is an unspoken assumption that the investments are about the same size. The results will differ if nine of the investments are $10,000 each and one is $100,000. Or if half are $25,000 in size and half $250,000.

With those assumptions exposed, let's go back to the table. In this successful portfolio, just one out of the ten investments has a 10x return. In reality, an investor's "home run" could be 12x or 20x or 100x, too, but 10x is the minimum for the following to be true: if 1 in 10 investments returns 10x, then that one investment has returned all the original capital from all ten investments. In other words, the portfolio is "repaid" by one investment. The other nine investments then determine the amount of total gains.

Looking at the second line of the table. Two of the investments have returned 5x. In reality, this could be anywhere between 2x and 7x. Investors may call these "doubles" (in keeping with the baseball parlance) or, for those investors who truly think every investment should be 10x, they'll call these returns "base hits," as if doubling your money is a bad outcome. (What happened to 8x and 9x? Those are close enough to 10x to get rounded up.)

Next we have three investments that return the original capital. A 1x return. It's not uncommon for these to be exactly 1x, not a penny more or less. The reason is that the preferred equity terms nearly always include a preference that repays investors before the founders, and thus when the startup isn't doing well, the investors often look for an acquirer at a price just sufficient to repay the investors.

The last row of the results are four investments that return nothing. Zero. Nada. Bubkis. Startup investing is risky. A lot of startups do not find enough customers, do not reach profitability, and run out of money, returning nothing to investors.

The weighted average of this sample portfolio is 2.3x. Change the 10x to a 17x and the average goes up to 3x. Lose one of the 5x's, and the average drops below 2x. In general, success is considered anywhere between 2x and 3x. So instead of the 10x we were dreaming of above when focused on a single homerun investment, the total return on a "successful" portfolio is closer to 2.5x. Upon success you turn $10,000 into $25,000, $500,000 into $1.25 million, or $7 million into $17.5 million.

7 OUT OF 1O LOSE MONEY

Before we take it a step further, note that in this successful portfolio, seven out of ten investments were failures. Four were zeros and thus complete failures. Three were 1x, which look much better than zeros, but as they typically take 3-5 years to return 1x, the investor would have been better off leaving the money in a savings account earning 1%.

This result of seven out of ten failures is considered a successful result. 70% failures, 30% winners. Perhaps this is why baseball analogies are so common, because in baseball a .300 batting average is considered good, and that is a 30% success rate, too.

The flip side of seven of ten failures is three of ten successes. Yea, successes! But before you accept this 30% success rate as sufficient, compare this result to other asset classes. How do you feel if your mutual fund reports that seven of its stock picks went bankrupt, with four returning nothing and three just barely returning your capital? Or imagine you are moving across country and get a call that the moving truck was in an accident. Seven of your favorite collectables were damaged, four a total loss and three recognizable but no longer of any value. Having a bad day?

Note, as well, that this is what a successful portfolio looks like for a professional venture capital fund or professional Angel investor. Emphasis on the word **professional**.

Professional. As in, their full-time profession is to make these investments. They turn down thousands of companies before picking any one investment. And after all their scrutiny, they invest only in companies that they think could return 10x. And yet they still only pick correctly 3 out of every 10 times.

What makes Sequoia, Kleiner Perkins, Andreessen Horowitz, Union Square, and my friend Geoff Entress so successful is that they review more opportunities than other investors and consistently choose one in ten investments that returns them 20x or 30x or 50x. But at the same time, even they still fail more than half of the time.

2.5X NOT 10X

Let's back to the portfolio analysis. What's most interesting is that startup investors repeat the term "10x" over and over again, but the actual goal is only **2.5x** (plus or minus a few tenths).

Not so long ago I was at an investor education event. A dozen speakers across four hours. Across those hours, the term "10x" was spoken at least a hundred times. Not five minutes went by without someone referring to a "10x return." Not once did anyone explain why the 10x was needed. Not even Geoff Entress, who was one of the organizers of the event and one of the speakers.

This is not an isolated incident. I've been to many Angel groups meetings and Angel conferences, and only once have I seen anyone talk about the fact that the 10x comes only one in ten tries.

The one exception was a presentation by Rob Wiltbank, a researcher from Willamette University. Rob is best known for the 2007 research paper, "*Angel Investing in Groups,*" which analyzed thousands of actual Angel investments. The weighted average of all of those investments combined was 2.6x.

The point of all this is that the true goal of startup investing is a 2x-3x "cash on cash" return on investment across a whole portfolio. The proverbial 10x is an interim step toward that goal, and the rarest of the expected outcomes across the whole portfolio.

STARTUPS VS. S&P 500

I'll repeat once more, startup investing is not in fact about a 10x return. That 10x is the tool needed to reach the true goal. The true goal is to earn a return on an investment that makes the investment a risk worth taking. Given that investing in startups is riskier than investing in public companies, the return on investment from investing in startups should be higher than investing in public companies. Substantially higher.

In the U.S., the most common benchmark for investing in public companies is the S&P 500. Thus, over any reasonably long period of time (e.g., ten years) a startup investment portfolio should have a higher ROI than the S&P 500. The historic average since the Great Depression for investing in the S&P 500 companies is around 7%. A 7% return compounded over ten years is a 1.8x cash-on-cash return. A 2.5x across the same time period is an 11% return. This is why 2.5x is reasonable rate of return for startup investing. 11% is a lot higher than 7%. Whether it is sufficiently higher to offset the added risk is up to the investor to decide.

What we do know, however, is that from 2003 to 2013, the

average venture capital fund did not beat the S&P 500, returning an average of only 7.4% (2.04x). By early 2016 the average had finally risen above the S&P 500 and was just over 10% (2.6x).

Finally, do note these are the average returns across the whole venture capital industry. In reality, nearly all that success was captured by the top 10% of the venture capital funds with about half the funds never beating the S&P 500 because they failed to find any 10x winner.

UNINVESTABLE

ANOTHER COMMON TERM you hear around startup investors is "**uninvestable**," typically used in the phrase "that company is uninvestable." As with the term "10x," the term "uninvestable" is also bathed in unspoken assumptions.

First and foremost is the assumption that every investment needs to have the potential to return 10x. Almost no startups have that potential. Few companies in the history of mankind have grown fast enough and big enough to return 10x to their investors.

To see why this is true, let's consider a corner bakery: A highly popular profitable bakery earning $1 million per year, with 10% **net margins** and thus $100,000 per year in profits. Let's say it cost $300,000 in equipment and other setup fees to open the bakery. If the founder tried to raise that capital from a traditional equity investor, the investor would buy around one third of the company for the $300,000. That would value the company at $900,000 (if one third is worth $300,000, then the other two thirds are worth $600,000 for a total of $900,000). To reach a 10x return, the bakery would have to grow to $9 million in value (10x the $900,000 valuation). Unless this bakery invented the next thing after sliced bread, growing its profits into the millions, there is no way a bakery earning $100,000 per year in profits would ever be worth anything close to $9 million. The bakery is thus, according to traditional investors, uninvestable.

Most startup companies are like this bakery. They need capital to start and to reach profitability, but, once profitable, they do not grow exponentially. They do pay all their suppliers, pay their employees' salaries, and provide **cashflow** to their owners, but do not double or triple in size year over year without replicating the whole business (which would require replicating the initial startup capital).

Traditional equity investors look down upon these companies. They can't make a 10x return and thus they are not even considered worth talking about. Some investors go as far as claiming these companies are not "startups," as that term is reserved for the companies that can potentially return a 10x.

In reality, startups fall on a broad spectrum, ranging from companies that will never be profitable, those that will only ever break even, companies like the bakery that can earn a nice living for their owner, companies that scale across a city or state earning millions in profits, and up to companies that earn 3x, 5x, 10x, 20x, and 100x for their investors.

Digging into that reality, one discovers that over 500,000 new companies are started in the United States each year. Of those, only about 2,500 (half of 1%) are funded by venture capitalists. The rest are funded by the founders, their friends, their family, home loans, and credit cards. The same research shows that about half of these companies are no longer in business after three years. That sounds terrible, and is terrible, but not as terrible as the 70% failure rate of the successful Angel/VC portfolios.

My takeaway from that research is that there are hundreds of thousands of successful startups that are ignored by Angels and VCs. And there are far more when you include the rest of world outside the United States. Many, if not most, of these companies are quite investable, just not using the structure of traditional startup equity that expects 10x returns.

"Uninvestable" comes down to the structure of the investment and thus the investment model of the investor, not the company. Every profitable company is in reality quite investable, given the right terms.

DEBT OR EQUITY

TALK TO TRADITIONAL startup investors and they'll all tell you that there are only two possible investment structures: debt and equity. The proverbial "they" say a lot that turns out to be wrong.

DEBT

Debt doesn't work for most startups for two reasons. Before explaining why, let's define the term **debt**. Debt is a loan from lender (investor) to borrower (company). The lender provides **$D** to the borrower in exchange for a promise to repay **P%** per year in interest for **N** months, plus repaying $D in that same time period.

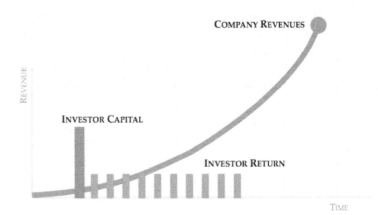

To make this concrete, think about a $100,000 loan with 5% interest repaid quarterly over 3 years. Such a loan would have 12 quarterly payments, each of $9,025.83. (Don't worry how to compute that value. Any of a thousand online loan calculators can compute the payment using nothing more than the size of the loan, the interest rate, the number of payments per year, and the total number of payments. Or, if you like spreadsheets as much as I do, you can learn how to use the =PMT () formula.)

Back to the two problems with startups and debt. First, startups that need money to grow usually can't afford the first few debt payments, as they have not yet grown their revenues. After the growth has arrived the payments become affordable, but it's a Catch-22 to get to that point.

Second, startups often fail. In the successful 10x investment model in the first chapter, seven out of ten investments failed. If seven out of ten loans fail, then 70% of the total expected repayments are lost.

To make up for those losses, the interest rate on the three good loans would have to be 25%-35% just to break even. Given that you can't tell which loans will success and which will fail, all the loans would have to have 25%-35% interest. Trouble is, 25% interest is too high for just about every startup, and thus at 25%, the odds are that 90% of the loans fail. If only one in ten loans pays back, then it would need to charge 50%-75% interest, just to break even.

This is an impossible, *vicious* cycle, as the higher the interest rate, the higher the odds of failure and thus the higher the interest rate must be. We see interest rates like this at banks in Latin America and Africa, for exactly this reason. And with interest rates so high we see very few loans to companies in those countries.

All this applies only to the "seed capital" needed to get a company up and running, not the "growth capital" needed to scale up a business that is succeeding. Once a startup has customers and revenues from those customers, then debt can make sense. Once a company has some operational history, it is possible to predict its cashflows and determine the risks of future cashflows. An investor can use this information to compute an affordable interest rate that works for the company, and which provide a reasonable return to the investors.

Do note that seed capital is often raised in the form of convertible notes, which look like loans. In reality these are not really loans, they are pre-purchases of future rounds of equity. For more details on convertible notes, see *The Next Step: The Realities of Funding a Startup.*

EQUITY

Traditional startup investors buy shares, a.k.a. **equity**. In particular, startup investors buy **preferred shares**. There are shares that are **preferenced** over the founders' **common** shares. In an equity investment, the investor provides $D to the company in exchange for S shares. Since the total number of shares is known, the amount of ownership purchased is often referred to as P% rather than S shares.

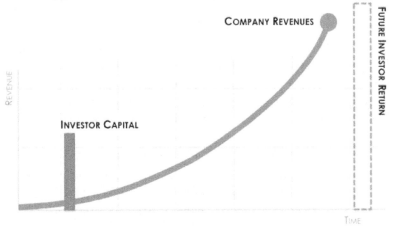

Unlike with debt, the company does not promise to make any payments back to the investor, nor does the investor expect any payments from the company while it is operating independently and privately.

For "venture scale" companies (i.e., companies that grow quickly enough to interest venture capital funds) the expectation is that there will be multiple *rounds* of investments every 12-18 months. Each round adds new investors and sells new shares, *diluting* existing investors' and founders' percentages ownership.

For example, back in the 1990s and early 2000s when I was co-founding software companies, my third startup, Medio, raised $750,000 in seed capital. Then, a year later, Medio raised $11 million in a *Series A*, and the year after that $30 million in a *Series B*. Ten years after starting that company, nine year after that Series A, five years after I had left to start a new startup, Medio was acquired by Nokia. Only then did the investors receive a return on their investment.

My next company was Ground Truth. It raised $2 million in its Series A, $7 million in its Series B, then merged with a competitor and raised an $8 million Series C. We parted ways after the merger and now nine years later the company has raised yet-more money from new investors, still operates, and is keeping its investors waiting for an exit.

Meanwhile, most startups are not venture scale, and as such do not have the option of raising round after round after round. They instead have to find a path to profitability using one or two smaller rounds of investment. But being venture scale doesn't guarantee three or more rounds. There are fewer Series B investments than Series A, and fewer Series C than Series B. Thus most startups face the difficult reality of having to become profitable before they run out of investment capital and are forced to go out of business.

For software companies, the one additional path to an exit is an *aquihire*, which looks like an acquisition, but is really a recruitment technique where a large company can hire the whole team from a failed startup, often at a lower price than hiring a recruiter, and often for less money than the investors invested. Everyone's resume looks better as they can claim the startup was acquired, and the investors get a 0.1x or perhaps even 0.5x instead of a total 0.0x loss.

No matter whether the exit is a 0x loss or a 20x gain, the key pattern to notice for equity investments is that the investors are promised nothing when they invest, and have no idea how long their capital will be locked up while waiting for an exit. Investors invest based on the hope that their capital will be used to increase the value of the company, and the hope that either that value is large enough for the company to go public or large enough to catch the interest of a larger, more established company.

In the U.S. tech sector, each year about 2,500 companies receive a Series A investment from a venture capital fund, and about 200 startups are acquired or go public. Most of the acquirers buying those startups are themselves former tech startups which succeeded wildly: Apple, Google, Microsoft, Facebook, and Cisco.

In the organic food sector, a dozen or so companies have managed to grow big enough to catch the attention of an acquirer, e.g., Stonyfield Farm, acquired by Danone; HonesT, acquired by Coca Cola; and Ben & Jerry's, acquired by Unilever.

In the media sector, the numbers are smaller still, with startups like C|Net and SportsLine both acquired by CBS, and The Huffington Post and TechCrunch, both acquired by AOL.

In other sectors, and outside the U.S., acquisitions are far less common and IPOs nearly unheard of, which is a problem for equity investing. Unless there are a lot of acquirers or an easy path to go public, investors are investing far too much in hope rather than in anything under their control or under the control of the startups.

This is why, when visiting any Angel group, you'll hear a lot of stories about the investments they've made, but very few stories about exits. Exits are rare, take a very long time, and do not happen on any predictable schedule.

ZOMBIES

Equity investments have one other all-to-common outcome. Rather than run out of money and go out of business, the startup can be profitable, but not earning enough money or growing fast enough to catch the attention of an acquirer and have no where near enough money to go public. These are the so-called *zombie* investments.

Zombies can be earning millions in revenues. Zombies can be profitable. The problem is that the value of startups comes far more from **growth** in revenues and profits. A company growing 100% or more per year has value. A startup that was once growing at that rate, whose growth slows to 20% per year has almost no value.

If a company's value is less than the capital provided by the investors, then the investors have no compelling reason to push for an acquisition. For VCs, it is better to have a 1x on the books than a 0.5x return distributed back to their investors. For Angels, there isn't much they can do to make an acquisition happen. The best they can do is keep up their hope that something good someday will come out of their investment.

From the point of view of the company, the founders may get frustrated that all their work will not be highly rewarded, but meanwhile their zombie company pays everyone's salaries, including theirs. As long as the company stays breakeven or profitable, it can stay in business, leaving the investors in a state of limbo for decades.

Back at those Angel groups, what frustrates the Angels the most are the companies that they invested in over five years ago, which are doing just fine, but it looks like there is no likely path to an exit. And unlike a venture capital fund, which itself has a 10-year expiration date, Angels are stuck with their investments until the companies go out of business or have an exit. Patience is a required virtue for equity investors.

INVESTING
IN
REVENUES

ALTERNATIVE INVESTMENT STRUCTURES

REVENUE-BASED BASICS

REVENUE-BASED FINANCING is not a specific investment structure, but instead a general theme. The concept can be applied to debt, to equity, to structures somewhere in-between, and to contracts that are neither debt nor equity.

CASHFLOW

Before diving into those details, let's start with the general idea: in exchange for **$D**, the company promises to pay the investor **R%** of the company's revenue, until **$X** is repaid to the investor.

Let's break that down. First, like in the preferred equity example in the first chapter, we have $D of cash. If you don't like abstract values like $D and prefer concrete numbers, think about a nice, round, $100,000 investment.

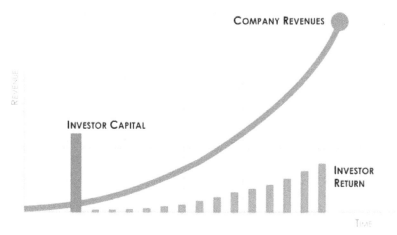

Unlike the preferred equity investment in Chapter 1, this time the company is promising to repay the investor. That promise isn't some fixed percentage of $D like in a traditional loan, but instead it is a percent of revenues. These "revenues" could be **"top-line revenues"** (a.k.a. gross revenue or gross receipts) or they could be **net revenues** after subtracting the cost of goods, or they could be **"free cash flow"** or **"profits"** however the investor and entrepreneur both agree to define those terms. Personally, I like top-line revenues and I'll explain why later.

The percentage of revenues is negotiable. For top-line revenues, it's typically a single digit value, i.e., 1%-9%. Later in the book I'll explain how to determine which value to use. For now if you want a concrete number, think 5%.

Lastly, there is the amount of money paid back to the investor, $X. Like in the world of 10x equity investing, we talk about this as a multiple of $D. This number can vary from 1.1x to 5x. Typical values are 2x for growth-stage investments, and 2.5x-4x for seed investments.

EXAMPLE

Below is a sample $100,000 investment. Given that each company grows at a different rate, and that the percentage of revenue can vary from deal to deal, other $100,000 revenue-based investments can look quite different. Furthermore, to keep the tables as simple as possible the cashflows are shown as annual. The frequency of repayments in actual deals varies, with most being monthly or quarterly.

REVENUE BASED FINANCING

Year	Revenues	Cash Flow
0		($100,000)
1	$200,000	$10,000
2	$400,000	$20,000
3	$480,000	$24,000
4	$640,000	$32,000
5	$720,000	$36,000
6	$760,000	$38,000
7	$800,000	$40,000
TOTAL	$4,000,000	$200,000
ROI		2x
IRR		17%

The table shows the annual revenues of the company and the cashflow from the company to the investor based on 5% of those revenues. The **Cash Flow** column shows the cash flowing from company to investor, thus the investment from the investor to the company is shown as a negative number (using the common accounting notation of parenthesis to denote negative values). This investment is listed as Year 0. If that is confusing, replace "Year 0" with "INVESTMENT."

Successful companies tend to grow their revenues year after year, and thus Years 1-7 show steadily growing revenues, and with that, steadily growing cashflow back to the investor.

The total revenue in the seven years is $4 million. Five percent of $4 million is $200,000, which is 2x the original $100,000 investment. These values are shown in the **TOTAL** and **ROI** rows. "ROI" stands for **"return on investment."** The ROI in this example is the so-called **"cash-on-cash return on investment,"** which ignores the fact that the value of a dollar changes over time due to inflation.

The other success metric in this example is a 17% IRR. IRR

stands for "**internal rate of return**." This is a fancy bit of financial jargon which (more than less) describes the equivalent interest rate you would have received if you had lent the initial capital to the company and they had paid you back at a fixed interest rate. The math to compute IRR is complicated, but we don't have to do that manually, as the =IRR() formula in a spreadsheet will compute it for us. In fact the reason the table above begins with the investment listed as a negative number is that the =IRR() formula requires that negative value to do its computation.

STRUCTURES

The above example shows the cashflow, but doesn't talk about the structure of the investment. What is interesting about revenue-based investments is they come in a variety of structures. The two most popular of these are revenue-based loans (debt) and revenue-based equity.

The choice of structure depends on the individual investment. Sometimes one choice is a better choice than the other, and sometimes what is ideal is something in between.

In all cases, the key variables are the percent of revenues and the multiple cash-on-cash return. But each structure can include many other terms and conditions to fine tune the deal.

REVENUE-BASED LOANS

THE SIMPLEST OF RBF structures is the revenue-based loan. In its ideal form:

- The lender pays $\underline{\$D}$ to the borrower
- The borrower pays the lender $\underline{R\%}$ of **quarterly** revenues
- Payments continue until a total of $\underline{\$X}$ is paid from borrower to lender

This is nearly identical to the description of the cashflows described above. The only important distinction is that the frequency of repayments is specified. The common choices for that are monthly or quarterly, but I have seen both weekly and annual payments used as well.

Unlike traditional debt, there is no timeframe stated for the total repayments, i.e., there is no "maturity date" for the loan. It gets repaid when R% of future revenues adds up to $X, however long that takes. From the investor's point of view, that is risky compared to a traditional loan, since the future revenues may be lower than expected. From the borrower's point of view, the lack of deadline is a benefit, since the payments are directly tied to the amount of revenues, thus ensuring that the payments are affordable. (Assuming R% is small enough compared to the net margins of operating the business that it is affordable).

REALITY BREAK: In the United States, due to the IRS tax code, revenue-based loans must have a stated interest rate and maturity date in order to be considered loans. The common fix for this is to use the published minimum interest rates and maturity dates far in excess of the expected repayment period. E.g., for the most recent 2x RBF loan that I negotiated, we expect to be repaid in five years, yielding 10% IRR. To comply with the IRS, the terms included a 1% annual interest rate and a maturity in 9 years, at which time any outstanding balance has to be repaid. I picked 9 years as the IRS sets minimum interest rates based on loans less than year in length, less than ten years in length, and longer. Hopefully someday the IRS will recognize the ideal RBF form so that we can simplify the paperwork to match the intent of the agreement.

A revenue-based loan can be as simple as the above example. Or, if the investors feel the need for additional risk mitigation or a greater return on investment, it can include any or all of the common preferences used in startup investing, many of which are described later in the book.

REVENUE-BASED EQUITY

REVENUE-BASED EQUITY is also rather simple. In its ideal form:

- The investor pays **$D** to the company,
  in exchange for **N** shares.
- The company agrees to repurchase **N** shares using **R%**
  of **quarterly** revenues at a price per share that returns **$X**
  to the investor.

This is again nearly identical to the description of the cashflows in the last chapter. Again, the frequency of repayments are specified. The two most common frequencies are quarterly and monthly, though they might also be annual. The key difference is that investors are buying shares in the company and are thus shareholders, rather than lenders, albeit only for as long as it takes the company to repurchase (a.k.a. "redeem") all those shares.

The number of shares makes little difference, except in the case where the company has an exit before all the shares are repurchased. In addition, when the investor is buying a specific number of shares (N), at a known price ($D), it is possible to calculate a valuation of the company. The value of **N** is thus typically chosen to make that valuation seem reasonable to the company, the investor, and any outsiders who might see the deal terms.

The paperwork for a revenue-based equity transaction can be derived from a common, off-the-shelf stock purchase agreement. It is basically a stock purchase agreement, but with some added language describing the obligation by the company to repurchase shares.

This is exactly how we created the Stock Purchase Agreement at Fledge, the conscious company accelerator I founded after leaving the world of venture-scale tech startups. I've seen the same from other startup lawyers in other RBF equity investments I've been involved in outside of Fledge. All these agreements include a few other important details:

ACQUISITIONS

What happens if the company is acquired before all the shares are repurchased?

In the Fledge Stock Purchase Agreement, upon an acquisition, the company is obliged to pay the investor the full $X. However, in the case where the value of the shares is greater than the amount of money to repurchase the yet-redeemed shares, the investor would instead be treated like any other shareholder and the shares purchased by the acquirer like any other shares.

In other words, the investor gets either whatever was originally promised or the value of the shares, whichever is bigger.

This is one of the advantages of revenue-based equity over revenue-based debt, as there is a potential to return more money than expected.

EARLY REDEMPTIONS

Does the company have the right to repurchase the shares early?

In most agreements, the answer is no (with one exception). The reason not to allow early redemptions is to avoid the case where the managers of the company know an acquisition is imminent, and so buy back the shares early to avoid sharing the windfall with the revenue-based investors.

The exception to this rule is when the company raises more money. For example, the Fledge Stock Purchase Agreement says that the company can repurchase any or all of our shares when raising a "significant" round of investment. We purposefully used the vague term "significant" because we need our agreement to work for hundreds of companies without customizing the values for each company. In reality, if the company is raising more than they owe Fledge, we're fine with them buying us out early.

As long as an acquisition isn't imminent, an early redemption is great for a revenue-based investor. The sooner the $X is returned, the higher the IRR.

PARTIAL REDEMPTIONS

It is possible (and common) for the company to buy back only some of the shares rather than all **N** shares.

In the Fledge Stock Purchase Agreement, the companies are obligated to buy back only **half** of Fledge's shares. We keep the other half in case any of our *fledglings* have a big exit. As deeply as we believe in revenue-based investments, we know that given 100 startup investments, the odds are that at least one will be a breakout hit. We don't want to miss that additional return on investment.

OPTIONAL REDEMPTIONS

It is also possible to make the redemptions optional for the investors. This allows a company to raise money from investors who like revenue-based investing alongside those who want the potential higher upside of equity investing, both at the same time, all using the same paperwork.

To do this, in the stock purchase agreement, the investor chooses whether to participate in the stock redemption or not.

To make this even more flexible, the company can let the investor choose a percentage of shares that are redeemed, e.g. 0%, 25%, 50%, 75%, or 100%.

And the company can allow the investors to update this choice over time. For instance, there might be a case where a company that at first seemed poised to be a huge success instead turns into a company that finds a niche and is profitable, but is not likely to be acquired or go public.

That is how the *zombie* investments are formed, and revenue-based investing provides a *structured exit* to investors, avoiding the creation of yet-more *zombies* investments.

REVENUE-BASED DIVIDENDS

ONE ISSUE RAISED for revenue-based loans and revenue-based equity is that the startups repay the investors before the startups are profitable. In addition, in the U.S., there are unanswered questions around whether revenue-based investments trigger an Original Investment Discount (OID), which complicates investors' tax filings. To overcome these issues, some revenue-based investors are using dividends to create their return on investment:

- The investor pays **$D** to the company, in exchange for **N** shares.
- The company agrees to pay **P%** of profits as **quarterly/annual** dividends until **$X** is provided to the investor.
- At that time, the company agrees to repurchase all **N** shares for the original **$D**.

Using this structure, 1x comes from the repurchase of the shares. Any additional return comes from any future profits, paid through dividends. The size and schedule of the dividend is specified in the stock purchase agreement, but, legally, the power to issue dividends comes from the board of directors. So in this structure, the investors need to have a seat on the board.

One variation I've seen in this structure is for the company to pay P% of profits for a specific number of years, rather than up to a specific $X. That provides an *upside* to investors in case the company performs better than expected.

REVENUE-SHARE

IT IS POSSIBLE to forgo all the trappings of debt or equity and structure the investment as a pure revenue-sharing agreement.

- The investor pays **$D** to the company
- The company pays the investor **R%** of **monthly** revenues
- Payments continue until a total of **$X** is paid from company to investor

This is nearly identical to the description of revenue-based debt. The difference is that this investment is not a loan. Corporate law and tax law include a large corpus describing debt, and bankruptcy law includes protections for debt holders. A revenue share as described above is a simple contract that does not come with any of those protections.

Investments of this form are commonplace in mining, oil, and movies. Investors typically buy a percentage of the gross revenues generated from those assets, or a percentage of the net revenues, with the deductions from the gross clearly spelled out in the contract.

Fledge used a structure like this for its experimental online program, charging the participants 1% of their next $2 million in revenues. The companies owed a $20,000 tuition, paid upon success, with $D set at zero. The investment we made was not cash, but instead our time and mentorship. We used this structure because it made the contract simple, just one page long, easy for the entrepreneurs to understand without paying a lawyer to revue the legalese of a promissory note or stock purchase agreement.

COMPARING STRUCTURES

THERE IS NO SINGLE revenue-based structure ideal for all situations. Each structure has its pros and cons, especially around expenses and taxes, and each structure has its best and worst case outcomes.

Revenue-based Structures			
	Debt	Equity	Dividends	Revenue share
Interest is tax deductible	✓			✓
Lower taxes for investors		✓		
Contractually guaranteed payments	✓	✓		✓
Upside beyond repayments		✓	✓	
Downside protection	✓			

Revenue-based debt is most commonly used for growth capital. For a company with growing revenues that is profitable (or soon to be profitable), a revenue-based loan can provide a simple structure with a fairly predictable return to the investors. The interest paid on the loan is considered an expense and thus tax deductible (in the U.S.). This makes the actual *cost of the capital* lower to the company than it seems at first glance. For investors, the interest is taxed as "ordinary" income, which (in the U.S.) is taxed at the highest rates.

Revenue-based equity is most commonly used for seed capital. For a company with no history of revenues, it is difficult to predict when the share redemptions will happen, and how long it will take for all the redemptions to finish. Such investments thus have the feel of a traditional equity investment. The difference is that with the revenue-based structure, the investor doesn't have to wait for an exit to start getting a return on their money. Revenue-based equity with a partial redemption mixes the repayments from redeemed shares with a traditional equity investment, all in a single transaction.

In terms of taxes, redeeming share is not considered a business expense (in the U.S.) and thus is not tax deductible to the company. All redemptions above and beyond the initial investment are *capital gains* to the investors, which (in the U.S.) are taxed at the lowest personal income tax rates.

Finally, revenue-share agreements are similar to debt. The revenue-share is an expense to the company. The income to investors is considered "ordinary" income.

UPSIDE AND DOWNSIDE

Unlike for traditional debt, revenue-based financing has no strict timeframe for repayments. Both the investee and investor estimate how long it will take for the repayments to occur. From that estimate, they can calculate an estimated *cost of capital* to the company and *return on investment* to the investor (which, except for taxes, are the same value).

In all cases, if the company grows its revenues faster than expected, then the repayments will come back sooner and the return on investment will be higher than estimated. Thus, all revenue-based investments have a potential *upside*.

Similarly, all revenue-based financings have a potential *downside*. This occurs if the repayments take longer than expected. Plus, of course, the worst-case *downside* is if the company goes bankrupt or goes out of business and stops making payments altogether.

For revenue-based loans and revenue-share contracts, that is the full extent of upside and downside possibilities. However, for the loans, in the worst-case the investors may get some of their money back when the company liquidates its remaining assets. This is because debt holders get paid back first when a company goes bankrupt or goes out of business.

For revenue-based equity, there is one other upside case. The company may exit before all the shares are redeemed. What happens in this case needs to be specified in the stock purchase agreement. For Fledge, our agreement states that upon a *change of control* of the company, the company owes either the amount still due through redemptions or the value of the shares as a percentage ownership of the company, whichever is greater.

For revenue-based dividends, the terms of the deal may include dividend payments for a specific number of years, rather than for a specific $X of cash return. A structure like:

- The investor pays **$D** to the company,
  in exchange for **N** shares.
- The company agreed to pay **P%** of profits as
  quarterly/annual dividends for **Y** years to the investor.
- At that time, the company agrees to repurchase the
  shares for **$D**, returning the original capital.

This created the potential for a large payout to investors if profits outperform expectations.

WHICH IS BEST?

As you can see, there is no one structure that is ideals for all investments. It isn't obvious which one is best for your next investment. And what might be best for the investor isn't necessarily the best structure for the company.

That said, for the early-stage impact investments that I've seen in the last half decade, the ideal structure is far more often one of these revenue-based structures than a traditional debt or equity structure.

HONEYMOON, ETC.

WHEN MAKING REAL-LIFE INVESTMENTS using revenue-bases investment structures, there are a few other common terms that get added to the agreements.

REPAYMENT HONEYMOON

It is not uncommon to include a *honeymoon* period, i.e., to start the repayments after waiting 6, 9, 12, or months, rather than starting repayments in the first month or quarter.

This makes sense when the company needs a few months before the investment capital increases their sales revenues. This is most obvious when that capital is being used to buy a piece of equipment, which needs to be ordered, installed, and integrated into production. Or when the capital is used to plant a crop of vegetables, which takes months to be ready for market. Or is used for marketing, to increase the pipeline of potential customers.

The difficult part is determining how long to set the honeymoon period. For young companies, it is always a challenge to predict future revenues. However, remember that in revenue-based financing, the repayments come from revenues, so if the actual revenues are less than predicted or take longer than expected, the repayments begin small, proportional to the early revenues.

GROSS VS. NET REVENUES

In revenue-based financing, the company pays the investors a percentage of "revenues." But which definition of revenues: gross receipts, net revenues after subtracting the cost of goods, after shipping and VAT? The definition is a key decision to be made in each agreement.

Most revenue-based financing uses a percentage of *gross revenues*. Of all the possible choices for defining "revenues," top-line, gross revenues is the one and only value in standard accounting that cannot be re-defined by management after the agreement is signed. Every other line in a financial report is decided (and thus controlled) by management.

Net revenues (gross revenues minus the cost of goods) is determined by what is included in the cost of goods. Determining whether an expense is a fixed or variable expense is not always clear. That choice doesn't make a difference to the bottom line, but it can make a significant difference to a revenue-based investor who is paid a percentage of "net revenues."

Free cash flow and *profits* are even more difficult to define. Are capital investments subtracted? Is depreciation added back in? Are profits computed before or after paying taxes?

To minimize the potential for misunderstandings and to keep the interests of investors and management aligned as close as possible, I highly advocate for the use of gross revenues in all revenue-based investments, not net revenues, not free cash flow, and not some other value that flows through the board of directors to become a dividend payment.

However, on occasion, "gross revenues" is not the right choice. For example, the crowdfunding website, Kickstarter, collects donations from thousands of crowdfunding campaigns, but keeps only 5% of the total collected revenue, passing the other 95% through to its customers (the companies/projects raising money). In this case, the terms for investors in companies like Kickstarter should state that the redemptions will be based on the *adjusted gross revenues*, defined as gross revenues minus the money passed to customers. This should be broadly defined, not specified as 5% of gross revenues, so that if the company needs to change its business model to change its model to share 98% of the money, the company does not have to worry that its revenue-based financing becomes unaffordable. Similarly, if the company is able to increase its share of the donations to 10%, the investors do not feel like they are being left out, or worse, feeling they were deceived in the financing negotiations.

REPAYMENT FREQUENCY

Are the revenue-based payments due monthly, quarterly, or annually? The right choice is dependent on both the company and its investors. I've invested using all three frequencies.

Monthly is nice, as it puts the company in the habit of making repayments to investors, lowering the chances that the funds are spent on unbudgeted expenses. However, a monthly frequency involves twelve transactions per year, twelve sets of paperwork, and potentially twelve bank wire fees.

I manage the portfolio for Fledge, and we've made dozens of revenue-based equity investments, plus have ten revenue-share contracts. Twelve times dozens is a lot of transactions, and thus I prefer quarterly payments.

In addition, many of the fledglings are overseas, in the developing world. The cost of transferring money from these countries is onerous. All of my overseas investments use a quarterly frequency to lessen these costs.

One of my investments uses a semi-annual repayment frequency, with the payments set in March and November. This odd arrangement is again in the agricultural sector, specifically, in Tanzania where there are two growing seasons of unequal lengths.

Two of my investments use an annual repayment frequency. Both of these investments are also in the agriculture sector, and in both cases the entrepreneur argued that the annual harvest season justified an annual redemption. Personally, I would have preferred quarterly, to avoid a long delay between harvest and repayments, and as an incentive for the entrepreneurs to provide quarterly progress reports vs. annual reports.

PREFERENCES

THERE IS MORE TO investment structures than how and when the cash is distributed from investor to company and back again. The rest of the details are outlined in the terms and conditions of the investment documents. Traditional equity investors use preferred shares, and thus the terms outlining the rest of the details are generally called *preferences*, no matter which investment structure is used.

Over the last half century, venture capitalists have developed a large collection of preferences, and Angels have adopted these in their seed investing as well.

Any and all of these preferences can be added to a revenue-based investment, whether debt, equity, dividend, or revenue-share.

Below is a short overview of each of these preferences. For more details, see Wikipedia and Investopedia.

BOARD SEATS

Management operates the company, and the board of directors manages the management team. Venture capitalists always ask for the board seat. Angels may or may not ask for a board seat, depending on the size of the fundraising and the size of the largest check.

Sitting on a board takes time and effort. It comes with some personal risk, as directors are liable to the shareholders for their decisions.

Companies rarely ask investors to sit on their board. Entrepreneurs tend to like to control their companies. Rather, the right to a seat on the board is a term included by the investors as a condition for making the investment. It is a demand by investors, with the negotiable details being the total size and composition of the board as a whole. (For example, three board members: one management, one investor, and one independent director).

APPROVAL RIGHTS

Investors may insist that specific actions made by the management team or board first require the investor's approval. Most commonly, these include: major changes to the business model; taking on a large debt offering; sale of equity; sufficiently large purchases; changes to the salary of managers; dividends; and the sale of the company.

In general, these are the types of approvals a board of directors is usually empowered to make. So investors require separate approval rights above and beyond the approval by the board, whether or not they also require a seat on the board. Some investors feel the need to enforce more control over the company, and these approval rights given them some control. Such approval rights are most commonly found in debt structures because it is less common for debt holders to ask for a seat on the board than it is for equity investors.

INFORMATION RIGHTS

Depending on where the company is incorporated, shareholders may not have a legal statutory right to review the corporate financial reports or to review the current *capitalization table*. (Also known as *cap table*, this is a table which lists the shareholders, their holdings, and their percentage of ownership). So the right to review this information, a.k.a. *information rights*, can be added into the investment documentation, granting these rights to the investors, and specifying when the reports will be delivered.

It has always seemed crazy to me that the owners of the company can be denied the right to know whether their company is profitable or not, how much money is in the bank, etc., and thus every investment I lead includes this preference.

A strict version of this right would require the company to deliver quarterly, unaudited financial reports (*Profit & Loss, Cash Flow*, and *Balance Sheet*) and an annual audited report. A less strict version would give the investors the right to review the corporate accounting books at any time, and oblige the company to deliver annual unaudited financial reports. In the U.S., auditing the financial reports costs tens of thousands of dollars, and thus is not often required for startups.

RIGHT OF FIRST REFUSAL / OFFER / LOOK

A *Right of First Refusal* gives the company the right to buy any shares offered by investors or employees, even if there is another buyer willing to buy those shares. This right allows the company to *step in front* of any transaction of its shares, and to buy all or some of shares being sold at the price negotiated between seller and buyer.

The purpose of this preference is to allow the company to control their shareholders. It is uncommon, but not unreasonable, for the investor to ask for this right as well. This would allow existing investors the ability to buy out other investors before the other investors sell to a new shareholder.

Two variations of this idea are often used to give similar rights to the investors: *Right of First Offer* and *Right of First Look*.

A *Right of First Offer* gives the investor the right to be notified whenever shares are being sold and to make a counter-offer. However, the buyer is not obligated to take that offer, even if it is higher in price.

A *Right of First Look* is simply the right to be notified whenever shares are being sold, and to be told the negotiated terms. This lets investors keep track of who their co-investors are. This right does not preclude the investor from making a counter-offer, but it does not hold up any transaction while waiting for an investor with a right of first offer to make a counter-offer.

PRO RATA RIGHTS

In venture scale companies, the historic pattern is three rounds of equity investments, each *diluting* the previous investors. Investors in venture capital funds do not like being diluted, and thus they insist on a right to participate in subsequent fundraising rounds with the right to buy enough shares in that round to keep their existing *pro rata share*, i.e., to keep their percentage ownership unchanged.

CO-SALE AGREEMENT

A *Co-sale Agreement* gives the investor the right to sell their shares whenever the company sells new shares. Generally there is a formula that specifies the ratio of shares an investor can sell compared with the number of shares the company is selling.

The purpose of this right is to allow an investor (or a founder, as this is a common term found in the shareholder agreements of founders' shares, as well) to *cash out* all or part of their investment when a much larger, often strategic investor wants to invest in the company.

This is also often found in regards to a company going public, in which case it allows the investor to sell shares alongside the company in the *initial public offering (IPO)*, rather than having to wait the 180 day (or longer) *lock up period* after the IPO, which is often listed in the stock purchase agreement, but which is there to comply with securities and stock market regulations.

DRAG-ALONG RIGHTS

Drag-along rights obligate the investors to follow-along when the majority of shareholders agree to sell the company or to go public. This protects the majority of shareholders from a minority shareholder who, for whatever reason, tries to block an exit.

THE NEXT STEP IN INVESTING

CALCULATING THE KEY TERMS

PERCENT OF REVENUE AND TOTAL RETURN

P% AND $X

HOW DO YOU pick the **P%** percentage of revenue, the **$X** return on capital and other terms of a revenue-based investment? You iterate through a few values in a spreadsheet until you find some everyone likes.

The process is not as hard as it may seem. Despite all of the above details, the vast majority of a revenue-based investment comes down to two numbers, **P%** and **$X**. The choice of debt or equity or dividends doesn't change this process. The cashflows in the process do not depend on how the investment is structured.

To start, you need a set of projections for future revenues. If there are any historic revenues, that is useful information, but if all you have are future projections, that is sufficient. To make this process less hypothetical, let's use the following example:

Year	Revenues	Growth
1	$200,000	
2	$300,000	50%
3	$400,000	33%
4	$500,000	25%
5	$600,000	20%
6	$700,000	17%
7	$800,000	14%
8	$900,000	13%
9	$1,000,000	11%
10	$1,100,000	10%

In this example, the company starts with $200,000 in annual

revenues, growing to $1.1 million over ten years. The round numbers are a bit contrived, but the basic idea of annual growth which slows year over year is a common pattern in actual startups (as opposed to the "hockey stick" growth patterns they all predict).

Usually the entrepreneur provides the revenue projections. These projects are based on their financial model. You can use those numbers directly in the initial revenue-based investment analysis to first see if the investment makes any sense at all. Then, if it does, spend the time to review the financial model. Do the due diligence to justify those values and see if they are reasonable expectations.

Once you have a set of revenue projections you are happy with, you can then compute a few different values of **P%** to see what each percentage of revenue could return to the investor. Don't worry about **$X** yet, the total returned capital, just pick a few values of **P%** and compute those values side-by-side. Below is 3%, 5%, and 7% of the above revenue projections:

Year	Revenues	Growth	3%	5%	7%
1	$200,000		$6,000	$10,000	$14,000
2	$300,000	50%	$9,000	$15,000	$21,000
3	$400,000	33%	$12,000	$20,000	$28,000
4	$500,000	25%	$15,000	$25,000	$35,000
5	$600,000	20%	$18,000	$30,000	$42,000
6	$700,000	17%	$21,000	$35,000	$49,000
7	$800,000	14%	$24,000	$40,000	$56,000
8	$900,000	13%	$27,000	$45,000	$63,000
9	$1,000,000	11%	$30,000	$50,000	$70,000
10	$1,100,000	10%	$33,000	$55,000	$77,000
		TOTAL	**$195,000**	**$325,000**	**$455,000**

This quick analysis alone is sufficient to see whether a potential investment is viable. For example, if the company was expecting to raise $200,000, you can see that 3% of their revenue stream over ten years of operations is insufficient to repay the original $200,000, and that 5% is insufficient to repay a 2x multiple on that investment.

If the expectation was that the investor would be repaid within five years, then the totals can be calculated across just the first five years to do the same quick analysis of affordability for a given **P%**.

But this is just a first-order analysis. To better see how the investment will perform, it helps to make this spreadsheet more accurate.

Year	Revenues	Growth	3%	5%	7%
1	$200,000		($100,000)	($100,000)	($100,000)
2	$300,000	50%	$6,000	$10,000	$14,000
3	$400,000	33%	$9,000	$15,000	$21,000
4	$500,000	25%	$12,000	$20,000	$28,000
5	$600,000	20%	$15,000	$25,000	$35,000
6	$700,000	17%	$18,000	$30,000	$42,000
7	$800,000	14%	$21,000	$35,000	$49,000
8	$900,000	13%	$24,000	$40,000	$11,000
9	$1,000,000	11%	$27,000	$25,000	$0
10	$1,100,000	10%	$30,000	$0	$0
		TOTAL	$162,000	$200,000	$200,000
			8.5%	15.2%	18.6%
			1.62x	2.00x	2.00x

First, include a time lag between earning the revenues and repaying the investors. For simplicity, I start with a time lag of a full year, and compute all the values on an annual basis. Only after I am satisfied with the results of the annual analysis do I re-compute the analysis for quarterly or monthly payments.

Back to the above example. Moving the revenue payments down to the following year leaves a blank value for year 1, which is a good place to include the invested capital ($D). Like in all the previous examples, let's use $100,000 for that value, and enter it in the spreadsheet as a negative number, i.e. "($100,000)." The parentheses are standard accounting notation indicating a negative number. The value is negative because the other numbers in the column represent cash flowing from company to investor and this investment flows the other way, from investor to company. Plus it is handy to start with a negative number because the =IRR() formula built into the spreadsheet expects the first item in the list of cashflows to be negative.

Second, add some formulas to the repayment cells so that the total in each column does not exceed the $X return of capital. In my spreadsheet, I do this by first computing the raw payments by percent of revenues (as seen in the previous table). Then in a separate set of columns, I use =IF(SUM()) functions in each cell to either copy the respective value from the raw payments table or to compute the final, smaller payment. You can see the result of that above in Year 9 of the column computing 5% and in Year 8 of the column computing 7%, as $25,000 and $11,000 respectively are smaller than the $40,000 and $42,000 in the previous spreadsheet. If you are not a whiz at spreadsheets, you can do this step by hand, deleting the cells that make the sum exceed $X and entering a final value to make the column sum add up to $X.

With the new table, it is now possible to see how many years it will take to return $X, assuming those projected revenues at a given P% of revenues. Plus, it is now possible to compute the IRR of the cashflows as well as the cash-on-cash return on investment (ROI).

For the above analysis, you can see that 3% of revenues only returns a total of $162,000 in 10 years. For a $100,000 investment, that is an 8.5% IRR and a 1.62x ROI. At 5%, a 2x ROI is repaid within 9 years and the IRR is 15.2%. At 7%, the 2x ROI takes just one year less, 8 years in total, but the IRR grows to 18.2%.

Ultimately all investments come down to "willing buyer meets willing seller," so there is no way for me to tell you if any of these results are viable or reasonable. Sometimes the first draft looks reasonable to both investor and company, and sometimes it doesn't.

If one of these columns does look reasonable, then the analysis spreadsheet can be used to fine-tune the estimates. For example, if the 5% column looks promising, then try changing 3% to 4% and change 7% to 6%, to see if either of those values look better. Or 4.5% and 5.5%, since there is no rule that says P% has to be a round number.

If all of the repayments take too long, then compute 8% and 9% of revenues. If that still doesn't work, then try lowering the amount of the investment, and have a discussion about whether the company is raising too much capital.

Sometimes the IRR is higher than it should be (given the stage of the funding and/or progress of the company). If so, then compute 1% and 2% of revenues, or try adding a honeymoon year 2 with no repayments.

HAPPY

If through this analysis you find a **P%** and **$X** that work, then the next step would be to go back and question the revenue projections.

NOT HAPPY

If, after trying every **P%** from 1% to 9% and every **$X** from 5x down to 1x, you are still not happy, then it is time to go back and question whether the company is truly viable.

What I have found in my experience is that if the company can't afford a revenue-based loan, then it is highly unlikely that the company can afford a traditional loan. If the company is projecting a steep "hockey stick" growth in revenues and yet the revenue-based analysis still doesn't work, then they are raising too much money, making the investment not viable for investors.

I have found myself in this position more than once after getting excited about an investment, only to discover that the numbers simply don't "pencil out" for investors. It makes for a tough conversation with the entrepreneurs, but no one ever said raising money was easy.

RE-PROJECTING

ONCE YOU ARE HAPPY with the P% and $X, it is time to go back and question the revenue projections. Research shows that only 1 in 300 financial models meets or exceeds their projections.

To account for this bias, make a copy of your analysis spreadsheet, lower the revenues, and see if the results are still reasonable.

For the projections we've been playing with, I made the following adjustments:

Year	Revenues	Growth	3%	5%	7%
1	$150,000		($100,000)	($100,000)	($100,000)
2	$200,000	33%	$4,500	$7,500	$10,500
3	$250,000	25%	$6,000	$10,000	$14,000
4	$300,000	20%	$7,500	$12,500	$17,500
5	$400,000	33%	$9,000	$15,000	$21,000
6	$500,000	25%	$12,000	$20,000	$28,000
7	$600,000	20%	$15,000	$25,000	$35,000
8	$700,000	17%	$18,000	$30,000	$42,000
9	$750,000	7%	$21,000	$35,000	$32,000
10	$800,000	7%	$22,500	$37,500	$0
		TOTAL	$115,500	$192,500	$200,000
			2.4%	11.7%	14.6%
			1.16x	1.93x	2.00x

Basically I took out a big chunk from Year 1, assumed it would take until Year 2 to reach $200,000 and Year 4 to reach $300,000. And as many companies hit a plateau of revenues at some point as they grow, I slowed down the growth after Year 8 as well.

With these changes, now 5% does not yet to a $200,000 return, even after 10 years, but at a 1.93x return of capital, the IRR is still 11.7%. The 7% column takes only one additional year for the full $200,000 return, with the IRR dropping from 18.6% down to 14.6%.

Again, I can't tell you whether these updated returns are reasonable or not. That is up to your appetite for risk and expectation of returns. What I can say is that the difference between 8 years and 9 years is small, and that if the investment will have monthly or quarterly payments instead of annual, the 14.6% will be higher if you calculate the cash flows month-by-month or quarter by quarter.

COMMON (MISGUIDED) OBJECTIONS

EXTRACTING CAPITAL

THE MOST COMMON objection of revenue-based investments by experienced, traditional equity investors is that the investors are extracting money from startup companies. Money that the company needs to grow.

Certainly they need capital to grow, otherwise they would not have raised money from investors in the first place. When raising capital, they promised their investors it would be spent wisely. On staff salaries, marketing, equipment, rent, etc.

No investor I've ever talked to objected to any of these other expenses. They found it totally reasonable that the employees get paid for their efforts. That the landlord get paid the rent. The phone companies for the phones. Etc.

So why shouldn't the capitalist be paid for the capital? When you boil down an investment, the return on investment paid to investors is the price paid for the use of the capital. It is rent, just like the rent paid for office space. Just like the hours-long lease for the use of an airline seat or days-long lease for the use of a rental car. The difference is that for historic reasons we call this particular rent either "interest" or "equity" and get confused as the product being offered, money, is also paid for in money, blurring the line between the product itself and the cost to rent that product.

In the 10x investment model, that cost of capital is quite high. $10 per $1 of investment. Again, this price is hidden, as it only shows up when an acquisition closes or when a company goes public, and at that same moment the founders are distracted by their own windfall, overlooking how expensive that seed investment turned out to be.

In a 2x revenue-based loan, the cost is a lot lower, $2 for each $1 of investment. $2 is only 20% the cost of $10. It is an 80% discount on capital. If there was a way to drop the payroll expenses by 80% (without sacrificing quality), any sane entrepreneur would do that. The same if the rent on office space could be slashed by 80%. Or a sale on office furniture, of computers, or whatever other equipment the startup needs.

In this case it is true that the $2 comes out of future revenues rather than some unknown date in the future upon an exit. Thus it is true that the $2 may be returned before the company is profitable. However, the company knows when it takes this capital how much of revenue must be shared and can account for that. If the company manages to hit its promised goals using the investors' capital, and if it pays them back as promised, odds are those investors and others like them are going to eagerly provide future rounds of capital to continue that success.

That is in fact how all future funding rounds happen, whether 10x or RBF. The company makes sufficient progress with the capital from one round to make its investors happy. They then provide capital in a subsequent round. Revenue-based investing doesn't change this at all, it just make the investors happier sooner, while lowering the overall cost of capital to the company. Win win.

LOSING OUT ON 10X

ANOTHER OBJECTION TO RBF by traditional equity investors is that if there is a big exit, the investors lose out on the big return.

If the deal is structured as a simple revenue-based loan or a simple revenue-share, then that is absolutely true. The same would be true for a traditional loan.

The same would again be true for a revenue-based equity or dividend-based investment, if the company can buy back all the shares without sharing any of the upside from the exit with the investors. There are two simple fixes for this.

First, investors can have the company buy back only a portion of their shares, keeping the rest in case there is an exit. At Fledge, we have our *fledglings* buy back half of our shares for this very reason.

Second, other preferences can be added to the stock purchase agreement. In the Fledge agreement, in the case of an exit the company owes us either the remainder of the repayments (i.e. they need to pay us the total amount for our redeemable shares minus what they've already paid us) or the value of those shares like any other Common shares, whichever is higher. This is similar to a 1x *liquidation preference* commonly found in traditional venture capital preferred equity investments, except in our deals we get the full 2x we were promised.

In either case, it is best to keep in mind how few startup investments ever exit at 10x or more. Fewer than one in ten venture capital investments do that well. Fewer than three in ten return 5x or more. It thus seems quite odd to me to structure all investments for the minority outcome, when instead it is possible to structure all ten investments in a form that all ten could return 2x or more.

IT'S COMPLICATED

I OFTEN HERE both investors and entrepreneurs tell me that no one has ever heard of these revenue-based structures. That it takes time to educate the other side of the transaction. That it is too complicated and too much effort.

That is a fair objection. It is absolutely true that 99.9% of investors and 99.9% of entrepreneurs have no idea these structures exist and thus no idea there is another choice beyond debt and equity. It is true that it is thus more effort to use these structures.

Short-term laziness, however, is not a good excuse for long-term happiness. RBF is a better structure for the entrepreneur-investor relationship, which is measured in years, not weeks. Investors say they invest in teams. An entrepreneur unwilling to learn about a better investment structure is raising a yellow flag of stubbornness. An investor unwilling to learn about a new structure is likely not the investor who will go the extra mile when something goes wrong, and at startups something always goes wrong.

I've discussed RBF with hundreds of investors and taught it at a dozen workshops. It is not rocket science or quantum mechanics. It can be summed up in a single sentence: *"You give money to companies and they pay you back a small percentage of their revenues until you double your money."*

It takes just as long to describe all the details of a preferred equity investment to a new Angel investor as it does to explain a revenue-based loan or revenue-based equity structure. It then takes a bit longer to explain how to find the right P% and to justify why the total return for that investment should be 1.7x or 2.0x or 2.5x.

Do note that this book itself is less than one hundred pages, and it didn't mention revenue-based investing for the first twenty pages.

REAL-WORLD EXAMPLES

FLEDGE

THE MOST COMMON structure I use is revenue-based equity through Fledge, my conscious company accelerator. In the first five years we've made more than sixty investments using a simple stock purchase agreement. The terms are not always identical, but the most common version is as follows:

Fledge provides $37,500 to the startups ($20,000 in cash plus $17,500 in services) in exchange for 6% of the total equity, provided to us as Common shares with three preferences.

First, the company is required to repurchase half of our shares using 4% of their future quarterly revenues, at a pre-determined price that totals $75,000. That provides a 2x return on investment for half of our shares.

Second, if the company is acquired before those shares are repurchased, the company must either immediately buy the rest of those redeemable shares, or if the value of those is higher, then we forgo the redemption and get paid for our shares like every other Common shareholder.

Third, the other half of our shares act like any other Common share, except that five years after signing the purchase agreement, we can ask the company to repurchase those share too, for whatever they are worth at that time, using terms to be negotiated at that time. This is not a common preference for starting investing, but allows Fledge to liquidate all of its investments so that it can neatly and cleanly end the lifetime of its funds.

Note that this structure is not optimized for each investee. There isn't time to do that within the format of a business accelerator, thus we picked terms that work for most startups.

ZIWETO ENTERPRISE

NOW THAT WE'VE seen the analysis for a hypothetical company, let's look a real world example: Ziweto Enterprise. This company participated in my Fledge accelerator in the seventh session, Spring 2016. At that time, they had three "agrovet" shops open in three rural towns in Malawi, providing veterinarian services and selling livestock medical supplies to rural smallholder farmers.

Malawi is one of the three poorest countries in the world. There are only a handful of foreign investors who have funded a startup in that country. There have been no "exits." It is thus a great place to do a revenue-based investment, as well as a country with pressing needs for just about everything, including what they sell at agrovet shops.

Five months after graduating, at the end of 2016, the Ziweto founders contacted me to tell me that Alfa Medics was for sale. This was the importer/distributor from which Ziweto bought 80% of the products for their stores. They told me they could acquire this profitable company for just $75,000, which was the value of the products sitting on the shelves in the Alfa Medics store, plus the value of the physical shelves. Alfa Medics was profitable, and thus with the purchase, Ziweto could leapfrog itself from a young aspiring startup to be a profitable company, lower the costs of operating their rural stores, and, hopefully, double the revenues of the combined company in one year.

The deal seemed too good to be true. After a few weeks of due diligence, it still seemed too good, but seemed to check out. Long story short, the previous owner was highly motivated, as he was from Tanzania and wanted to move back home, and finding any buyer in Malawi is a challenge, let alone one that fit his business exactly.

Fledge had already invested $37,500 into Ziweto using a revenue-based equity structure, and that investment was not even a year old. The simplest path forward was to tear up those terms and combine that $37,500 into the new $75,000 for a total of $112,500 with a new **P**%, a new **$X** and new terms and conditions.

More specifically, Fledge's investments are typically $37,500 in cash and services in exchange for 6% of the Common shares, with the company repurchasing half of those shares from investors using 4% of quarterly revenues for a total of $75,000. (By now you should be able to parse that sentence and understand the pieces.)

Because we were not expecting to bring in any new investors into this deal, the acquisition of Alfa Medics would not change the ownership percentages of Ziweto, and thus we decided to keep as equity the 3% equity from the original investment that isn't redeemable, structuring the $112,500 investment as a revenue-based loan. Assuming the enlarged Ziweto would be profitable, using the debt structure lets Ziweto count part of the repayments as an expense, which lowers their taxes. The loan form also saved us the trouble of having to figure out how many more shares to issue Fledge only to have those shares redeemed. We do not expect the expanded Ziweto to itself be acquired, as we know of no larger agrovet companies in Malawi or in Southern Africa that could afford to buy Ziweto, nor have we ever heard of a foreign company acquiring a company in Malawi.

Jumping into the revenue analysis, the Ziweto team had provided the financial reports from 2016 for both their existing company and Alfa Medics, with projections for 2017 and 2018:

Year	Revenues	Growth	5%	7%	9%
2017	$344,000		($112,500)	($112,500)	($112,500)
2018	$480,000	40%	$17,200	$24,080	$30,960
2019	$484,000	1%	$24,000	$33,600	$43,200
2020	$490,000	1%	$24,200	$33,880	$43,560
2021	$495,000	1%	$24,500	$34,300	$44,100
2022	$500,000	1%	$24,750	$34,650	$44,550
2023	$500,000	0%	$25,000	$35,000	$18,630
2024	$500,000	0%	$25,000	$29,490	$0
2025	$500,000	0%	$25,000	$0	$0
2026	$500,000	0%	$25,000	$0	$0
			$214,650	$225,000	$225,000
			14.6%	20.3%	24.9%
			1.91x	2.00x	2.00x

The Ziweto team did not try projecting revenues for 2019, so in my analysis I simply filled in a tiny growth rate until revenues reached $500,000, then left all future revenues at that value. I actually think it is more likely that the revenue could continue to grow beyond $500,000, but if the investment made sense with these values, then that leaves some upside if the business exceeds those expectations.

My goal was a 2x return, matching the 2x we use for the initial Fledge investment. When I talk with dozens of early-stage investors, I hear that 2x is the most common value they pick.

The 5%, 7%, and 9% values are the first values that I tried. Given 5% wasn't able to return 2x, and given the 25% IRR from 9% seemed too high, I focused my effort on 7%.

At this point I went back into the financial model Ziweto had provided, and plugged a 7% revenue share into their Profit & Loss statement. Their projected net margins were around 20% and thus 7% seemed quite affordable to the company.

Happy with that, I went straight to re-projecting revenues.

Year	Revenues	Growth	5%	7%	9%
2017	$200,000		($112,500)	($112,500)	($112,500)
2018	$300,000	50%	$10,000	$14,000	$18,000
2019	$400,000	33%	$15,000	$21,000	$27,000
2020	$490,000	23%	$20,000	$28,000	$36,000
2021	$495,000	1%	$24,500	$34,300	$44,100
2022	$500,000	1%	$24,750	$34,650	$44,550
2023	$500,000	0%	$25,000	$35,000	$45,000
2024	$500,000	0%	$25,000	$35,000	$10,350
2025	$500,000	0%	$25,000	$23,050	$0
2026	$500,000	0%	$25,000	$0	$0
			$194,250	$225,000	$225,000
			11.0%	16.6%	19.8%
			1.73x	2.00x	2.00x

Alfa Medic's revenues alone were $200,000 in 2016, so I started with a pessimistic assumption that it would take the Ziweto one full year to learn how to operate the bigger business. I then jumped revenues up to $300,000, which at 50% year-over-year seemed fast enough, despite Ziweto projecting that they could grow revenues to $340,000 in their first year of operations (2017). Finally, with no further projections provided by the Ziweto team, I went back to my method of year over year growth through 2022 to $500,000, as that would be quite a nice size company for Malawi, and as that leaves plenty of upside to this model.

Compared with the first analysis, the time to total repayment for 7% and 9% of revenues extends for only one extra year. The IRR at 7% of revenues drops from 20% to 16% and at 9% drops from roughly 25% to 20%.

The cost of capital from banks in Malawi for this type of deal is an annual fixed interest rate of 30%-36%, and thus a cost of capital of 16%-20% is a good deal for the Ziweto team. Given the track record of Alfa Medics' business, 16% seemed a quite reasonable return to me for the risk of this investment, including the risk of investing in Malawi.

All my overseas investments are in dollars, and thus Ziweto is taking on the currency risk. Historically, the Malawi Kwacha drops in values to the dollar every year, but far less than 10% per year, and thus the true cost of capital to Ziweto is still likely less than they can get locally (and in reality the banks wouldn't lend them $75,000 because banks don't lend against inventory, and those shelves we bought are the only other asset of the company).

The final signed deal was a revenue-based loan for $112,500, repaid quarterly at 7% of revenues, capped at $225,000 in total repayments, plus the 3% of non-redeemable equity from the initial Fledge investment.

GEOSSY

SOMETIMES THE TERMS are not as simple as **P%** and **$X**. Geossy is another graduate of Fledge, from the same session in 2016 as Ziweto. Geossy is a fish farm and supplier of baby fish and fish feed to other fish farms in Eastern Uganda. The company was two years old, bootstrapped, and profitable when they joined the Fledge program. They were seeking $200,000 in growth capital.

This deal was led by an African venture capital fund. Their lengthy due diligence included multiple site visits, in addition to analysis of the historic and projected financials. From that work, the venture capital fund determined that the right amount of capital was $170,000, and that the best structure was a revenue-based loan.

This was to be the VC's first revenue-based loan. So, to offset the risks of the variable payments, they decided that the payments should be monthly, and that they should include a fixed payment along with a variable payment:

Year	Monthly Payment
Year 1	2,083 USD + 2% of revenue
Year 2	8,250 USD + 5% of revenue
Year 3	8,250 USD + 5% of revenue

The reason for the lower payments in Year 1 is that it takes nine months to raise eggs into fish ready for the market. Projections were for the loan to be fully repaid by the end of the third year, with the total payments negotiated to be $289,000, a 1.7x cash-on-cash return on investment.

As often is decided with first-time investors and first-time entrepreneurs, the investment was split into two *tranches*, i.e. two separate investments within one round of investment. The two investments are separated by time, with a set of negotiated milestones to trigger the second payment. Tranching the investment allows the investor to build up trust and also provides some protection for the second investment in case something was missed in the due diligence process. The first tranche was to be $100,000 and the second $70,000, delivered upon reaching specific milestones. Also as happens with venture capitalists, the investment included most of the preferences described earlier in this book.

The use of past tense is not because the deal closed in the past, but because in the 11th hour, the venture capital fund backed out of this deal. Africa Eats (one of the Fledge follow-on funds) had agreed to be the co-investor in the deal, so we picked up the lead position and made three big changes.

First, we like quarterly payments, since that is one fourth as much paperwork per year as monthly payments. We adjusted the language to require Geossy to create a bank account and make monthly deposits, but to send us those payments only once at the end of each quarter.

Second, working side-by-side with our entrepreneurs in our accelerator, we build up a lot of social capital and trust, and thus we pared down or removed many of the preferences.

Third, we had expected to provide only $25,000 of the initial $100,000 tranche. The 11th hour was in reality more like the 13th, as the closing was a month behind schedule, so we didn't have time to gather a collection of co-investors. In the end we managed to close most of the first tranche two days after the VC decided not to do the deal with Geossy and us. We do expect to reach the full $170,000 once the first set of eggs has been raised and sold as fully-grown fish. Six months later, Geossy was able to buy more equipment with the first tranche than expected, the fish are growing, and the results from the first quarter of 2017 show the company should grow at least 40% relative to 2016, if not more.

APPENDIX

FURTHER READING

ONLINE CLASSES, MORE BOOKS, AND MORE ADVICE

lunarmobiscuit.com

MORE BOOKS IN THE NEXT STEP SERIES

The Next Step: *A Guide to Startup Sales and Marketing*
The Next Step: *A Guide to Building a Startup Financial Plan*
The Next Step: *A Guide to Pitching your Idea*
The Next Step: *The Realities of Funding a Startup*
The Next Step: *A Guide to Dividing Equity*

OTHER RECOMMENDED BOOKS

Venture Deals: Be Smarter Than Your Lawyer and Venture Capitalist
by Brad Feld and Jason Mendelson

ACKNOWLEDGMENTS

THANK YOU TO Gifford Pinchot III, co-founder of the Bainbridge Graduate Institute (merged into Presidio Graduate School, _presidio.edu_), for his foresight into the future of entrepreneurship and his openness to my mind's wanderings.

Thank you to the staff, fellow Entrepreneurs in Residence, and researchers at the University of Washington's CoMotion center for impact and innovation (_comotion.uw.edu_) for all your feedback.

Thank you to the team at Impact Hub Seattle (impacthubseattle.com), who have created a true community space that brings together hundreds of impactful entrepreneurs.

Thank you to the "fledglings" of Fledge, the conscious company accelerator (fledge.co), whose questions on entrepreneurship repeatedly demonstrate the complexity of turning ideas into startups.

And most of all, thanks to my brilliant wife and editor, Monica Aufrecht, who relentlessly ensured my words matched my thoughts and that those words would be understandable to you without the aid of a business school education or a business jargon dictionary.

ABOUT THE AUTHOR

MICHAEL "LUNI" LIBES is a twenty-plus-year serial entrepreneur, most recently founding Fledge LLC, the conscious company accelerator. Fledge helps entrepreneurs who aim to do good for the world while simultaneously doing good business.

fledge.co @FledgeLLC

Luni is an Entrepreneur in Residence and Entrepreneurship Instructor at Presidio Graduate School, advisor to The Impact Hub Seattle, and to a dozen startup companies. He is also an Entrepreneur in Residence Emeritus for the University of Washington's CoMotion center for impact and innovation.

presidio.edu

comotion.uw.edu

thehubseattle.com

Luni began his career in software, founding and co-founding four startups and joining a fifth. These include: Ground Truth (mobile market research and analysis), Medio Systems (mobile search and advertising), Mforma (mobile gaming and applications), 2WAY (enterprise collaboration systems), and Nimble (pen computing, PDAs, and early smartphones).

This book, the whole *Next Step* series of book, Luni's online classes, and other writing can be found at lunarmobiscuit.com. *@Lunarmobiscuit.*

INDEX

Made in the USA
Monee, IL
27 October 2021

80457671R00056